THE
THREAD

THE THREAD

A Journey through Trauma,
Healing, and Awakening

Lesley Gorrell

NOMANI PRESS

Nomani Press,
Galion, OH

Copyright © 2026 by Lesley Gorrell. All rights reserved.

No part of this publication may be reproduced, stored in a retrieval system, or transmitted in any form or by any means (electronic, mechanical, photocopying, recording, or otherwise) without the written permission of the author and publisher.

Library of Congress Control Number: 2025927012

Paperback ISBN: 979-8-9933188-0-6
eBook ISBN: 979-8-9933188-1-3

Book cover and interior design by Erin Seaward-Hiatt
Editorial production by KN Literary Arts

For all of us

Like the lotus, we too can rise from the mud, bloom out of
darkness, and radiate into the world.

—Unknown

Perspectives

I invited honest reflections from family, friends, coaches, therapists, fellow authors, and those whose lived experiences mirror my own. This is what I heard:

This is art.
Your book is what the world needs.
An unwavering commitment to the truth.
No one wants to hear this.

You are going to help so many people.
Every therapist's office should have a copy.
An urgent call for awareness.
You can never publish this book.

It's a lot of people's stories and should be talked about
    more.
Your poetry is powerful.
A compelling and necessary body of work.
You can't say these things.

It transcends into release, healing, and freedom.
Each line carries weight.
Your voice is strong. Your words matter. Keep going.
Silence . . .

Contents

Author's Note

This book explores themes of violence, sexual abuse, sexual assault, dissociative states, and self-harm. While its overarching intention is to uplift and empower, some of its passages may evoke difficult emotions.

If you feel the need to pause, please honor that need. Return when you feel grounded, safe, and ready to reconnect.

INTRODUCTION

Welcome. I'm so grateful you're here.

This book is for you. For me. For the collective. For the weight we've carried. For the words we could not find. And for those who seek to understand.

There is a thread that runs through all of us—an invisible yet undeniable connection that ties us to one another through our stories and our longing to reach the light beyond the darkness.

I didn't intend to write a poetry book. These poems came through me—more like a stream of consciousness than deliberate action. They emerged when I finally found myself in a safe enough place to hear them. Writing them was revealing and cathartic. Over time, several of them formed into this collection, though many more remain.

My purpose in sharing them is simple: I hope they reach someone who needs them.

The Thread speaks to our shared humanity, to the wounds that shape us, and the ways we mend. It is a journey that moves through the raw terrain of trauma, the ongoing process of healing, and the profound awakening that comes when we remember who we are.

Whether you find solace in the words themselves or in the simple knowing that others have walked—and are walking—this road, too, let this book serve as a reminder: You are whole, you are worthy, and there is hope.

May these poems hold space for you and reflect that healing is not only possible—it is yours.

LOVE AND LIGHT,
Lesley

The Messaging

~ remember who you are ~

Lesley Gorrell

Silenced

We aren't supposed to talk about this

Many won't understand
Or don't want to hear

It's okay . . .

We're not telling *them* yet
Only those who are ready to listen

Programming

Does he see me
Standing here
In front of him
Needing to be his victim?

I don't know how not to be
I always knew
What to expect

It wasn't intentional
But I got the message

Men
Wanting my body
A coveted object
And they hold all the power

Isn't our subconscious
Always seeking ways
To validate our beliefs?

Adults with good intentions
Warning children of things to fear
Hoping to keep them safe from the world

It's programming them
The way it all works
What to expect
What to believe

Where else could they end up
When they are taught
To fear the world
And all men in it?

That they are deviant
Somewhere inside
Wanting what they shouldn't have
In ways they shouldn't want it

So they have to hide
And plot
And sneak
And prey
On the weak

You know . . .
All the girls like me

Beckoned

Come here, girl
I want a piece of you

Isn't it true
That's what you're good for?
A place for me to lose myself

I mean anyone else would really do
Nothing special about you

You just happen to be the one
Standing in front of me

Lesley Gorrell

Object

Funny
How you can only see
Part of who I am
Whatever serves you
In the moment

I wonder if you feel regret
At least about those you are betraying
By being here

I'm mostly invisible
You see what you want
And leave the rest of me

I don't even count
It wouldn't even matter
Until I matter to myself

In this space
I'm consumed by you
I can't even breathe

When you're done
I don't even care
I could be anywhere but here

Listless
Under the weight of you
Surrendered
Under the spell of you

You're so quiet when it's over
Not another care

You're not even aware
Of who you are

Lesley Gorrell

The Huntsman

You are the hunter of bodies and souls
You are the hunger for control

I am the delicate bird on a wire
Always the object of your desire

You will take me however you can
The worst of a man

Moving through space
One thing on your mind

Scouring through
Picking the next prize

I will let you dominate me
I lost the power to disagree

Long ago

Robbed

Are you ready?
I can go for hours

You are here for me
To do what I command

I see your face frozen
Eyes wandering
Breath holding

Waiting
For what I will make you do to me

I can't wait
To take it all in

Everything I want to feel
Everything you don't want to give
I am taking

Lesley Gorrell

Two Truths

My truth
The shame
The game of who will and won't believe me

Yours
You really don't believe you did anything wrong

Scars

Sharpening their gaze on me
Deepening their resolve for me
Justifying their intentions to me
Widening their eyes at me

Expelling their breath on me
Fixating on the thought of me
Sweating their poison onto me

Writing the book of their life on me
My scars are their stories
That lied to me about who I am

Lesley Gorrell

Childhood

Bubble gum, bubble gum
In a dish
How many pieces do you wish?

Blood in my mouth
Blood on your hands
I can't stand this

The shift
How quickly things change
Behind closed doors

Something came over you
I watched as your eyes turned you into someone else

Innocence
Incidents we will never speak of

Silent truth
Palpable in this room

I will never utter a word
Neither will you

We don't have a clue what just happened

Perpetrator

Anything to get to your soft inside
Anything to win the prize
Access however I can get it
I don't really need your permission

I mean, if you give it that's fine
But it's a much better time
If I have to work for it

It's fun for me when you say no
I sit back and watch the show
I like a bit of struggle
No desire to take it slow

Fuck that shit
I hate being gentle
I just want to get down to it

It feels so good when you get me off
And I like you being distraught

It's a little funny
Not "ha-ha" but how it feels in my stomach
A little sickening
But a whole lot of "Yes, I'm winning!"

It's satisfying, violating you
You don't have a clue what I could really do
It may be worse for the runner-up
If I get bored

I might be more creative next time
Might need more to feed my mind
Goddamn, these cravings are strong
All rationale is gone

I like holding your arms
Maybe later I'll tie them up
Girls like you like a good fuck
Especially when it's rough

Do you like being punished
With all my pain?
Doesn't matter—I can't contain it
You're gonna need a rape kit

Wait
My gut is churning
I might have to vomit
That won't stop me from pushing through
Still on top of you

I have to keep going
So I have control
No time for a conscience
I'm on a roll!

Squeezing and crushing you
Like you are nothing
Well really, it's true
Know how I know?

'Cause you're gonna spend your whole life
Feeling that way
The piece of you I took today
The part that thought you may be worth something
Let me assure you you're not

That's the lesson you're getting from
This interesting twist
How crossing my path will change yours forever
God, I'm clever!

No one is ever going to call me out
I've sown the seeds of doubt
So you will never speak of this

I'm a goddamned genius!
Nothing ever between us
No one would believe it
Even if you squealed like a pig

Funny choice of words
That's how you think of us
All men grouped into one
We are never to be trusted

Well you sure as fuck got that right
Proved it to you tonight!

How can someone I don't even know
Do this to me?

Well, dear
Because you're just an object
My desire, a way to release
Don't bother calling the police

No one will think I did it
Well, anything wrong that is
Because they get it

It's in them too
Entertaining the thought of you
Innocent and broken
And crying and choking

They're just gonna turn
Another blind eye
Because they can't face me
Without facing themselves

Lesley Gorrell

Questioned

Sometimes poetry
Sometimes prose
You know how it goes

Rape of my body
Rape of my brain
It's the same

I don't give a fuck how he entered me
By force or by fear
I'm still processing all these years later

I knew I was in trouble
Frozen
Unable to move
Ever happen to you?

I finally reported it
The whole story
All they wanna know is
"Did you say no?"

To what?
He didn't fucking ask me anything!

"Did you fight back?"
It's not really a crime if you indicate otherwise

Fuck all of this
And fuck all of you
Who don't have a clue

The rest of us do

The Wounding

-remember who you are-

Lesley Gorrell

Curious

What a story to tell . . .

I wonder who will listen

Punishment

On the stairs
Bargaining
Bleeding from the knees
How did I get here?

Upside down
Swirling around
Tumbling in my mind
I can't see from my eyes

Don't do this
I'm begging you!
Someone please save me!

I should have chosen better than this
This is what I get
Somehow, I extended the invitation

The smell of this carpet under my cheek
Burning skin on my feet
Raw
Rubbed away from the pulling

It does not get lower than this
I can't go on

Lesley Gorrell

Please leave me here
Leave it all for me to swallow
I should have learned my lessons
Like a good girl

Leave me here in it
Spitting and screaming and sweating and dying inside

Let me die here
Not soon enough
I'm desperate for the end

Peace, please come
Please come now!

On the floor
Out of tears
Weakened from writhing

I'm slowing
I'm resigned
So quiet
So still

Waiting, hurting
Holding, suffering
No longer yearning for
The rescue that will never come

I feel everything
I hear the breathing
Until the poison is deep inside me

And I will be sorry
On the other side of this
For not being any better
I must have deserved it

And I will learn to live
Wishing it away

Dear Heavenly Father,
I'm coming to you . . .
In my dreams

Lesley Gorrell

Disconnected

Trapped
In my body
Here in the dark

Fingers squeezing on my skull
I can taste the pillowcase

Your arm on my neck
Smashing so hard
I can't feel my face

Smothering
Clutching
Holding
Squeezing
Spilling my silent tears

Anticipating
Bracing
Spiraling, into another world

I won't give you the satisfaction
Of begging you to stop
My God, please! in my mind
Praying on my knees

My shoulders are burning
My arms ripping away
Your grip is strong

You command, "Don't move"
As if I could

My head hurts now
I felt the snap
Disconnected
Something's happened

I like the buzz
Ringing in my head
Deafening
From the inside

I like spinning
I like floating
It's so easy
Compared to you

Lesley Gorrell

Without a Trace

You'll have me from behind this time
Just the way you like it

When you don't have to see my face
You've never seen a trace of me

Clueless

When I think love is letting you have your way with me

When you have no clue I'm not into it

Lesley Gorrell

Juxtaposed

We're the same
Don't you know?
Here to grow
Here we go

You—in my mouth
I'm wondering how I got here

Your hand—behind my head
Making sure you get deep enough
To get what you need
My eyes might as well be bleeding

I can't believe what I see
I can't believe what I feel
I hate this moment

We're the same
But so different

Chasm
Orgasm

What the actual fuck
Is going on here?

If opposites attract
It's true

You loving me
Me hating you

You hurting me
Me holding on

You sweating
Me retching

You standing
Me kneeling

Opposite feelings

Pleasure and pain
One suffers
One gains

I just don't know
How we can be

The same

Lesley Gorrell

Boyfriend

You're clicking the gun
You're telling me how
You're telling me now

Demanding my words
Or you're going to die
Suicide

You're crying your tears
You're telling me why
You need to hear my voice
To talk you through
What you can do to yourself
On the other end of the line

Desperate
Broken
Pleading

You're always needing
Another piece of my soul

The minutes feel like hours
Boulders crushing my chest

Hot sword slicing open my belly
Thick glue binding my tongue

Why can't I hang up this phone?

I can't speak
I'm paralyzed and choking

Still
Heavy
Holding
Waiting

For this to end

Lesley Gorrell

Waiting for Rescue

Under the radar
I'm flying
Beneath my covers
Crying my eyes out

I weep
I weep for it all

The bravest face for the world
The deepest pain
Of a girl reaching for answers

When will they come?
Who is the one who will save me?

Situations

It's all fun and games
Me being a girl
And everything you can do to me

Isn't this fun?
The way I play
And you thinking I like the way you move behind me?

I'm an actress in this moment
Someone else
Everything you want me to be

My sounds
My moves
The way I look at you
Making you believe . . .

The mood comes over you
Every chance there's no one looking

Except maybe your friends
But they're into it too
Cheering you on

Cheshire fucking grin on your face
It's just another day
Of seeing who and how far you can get

One more now
With your hands holding my hips
You can add me to your list

Mine is long too
I do what it takes to survive
I never wanted to be that way

How do you explain it?
Situations you don't want to be in
Time and again

Would anyone understand?

Alone

Hands around my neck
I know you love me

Palms and fingers squeezing my face
I know you want me

Your voice
Your breathing in my ear
I know it's all for me

Push your pain into me
I can take it

I'm so much stronger
Than you will ever be

I will just float away from you
And you won't even know

That you're alone here
In these moments

Lesley Gorrell

Resigned

I am slowing
Lying here

Knowing that I can't take much more
Of you all over me

I don't even care anymore

I'm so tired of this ride
Let's say good night
Forever

Let's go to sleep
And let it all go

Never knowing
If it could have been any better

Sleepless

I can't sleep
I'm waiting
To feel the squeeze

Crushing of my wrists
Rubbed raw
With your grip

Or rope
Or both
I welcome the burn

I'm almost relieved
When it's time
I need to get this over with

So I know
I'm allowed
To close my eyes
Without punishment

Sleepless
I'm so tired now
Almost worse than the torture
That's become comfortable somehow

I have to feel it
All the way
To know it's okay
For my eyelids to fall
Without interruption

You tell me "You're not done yet"
Letting me know
There's more to endure

Just go on
I'm not really awake anyway

Altered

I'm waiting for more
Not wanting to
But knowing I will go again
When you call me

I hate your voice
It's never nice
But I listen
Waiting for you to say . . .
Whatever it is

It doesn't matter
And on we go

Your hold on me
Something I can't understand

We're playing to lose
Every single time
I don't know why I can't turn away

You're ahead of me in this game
Let's call it what it is

Lesley Gorrell

Your hands on my hips
Pushing hard into me

My course has been changed
There I go
Never the same

Drifting

I found a way to escape you

Into the air
Outer space
The safest place
Only the light from the stars

How far will I go this time?

How long will it take
Before I find my way back to reality?

Lesley Gorrell

Survival

I'm your favorite ride
Up and down
Side to side
Round and round
Anything you like

I'll give you whatever you want
As long as it's over soon

I don't want to die
But die inside every time

I know how to survive
The games I play
To stay safe

As much as I can be
With a man like you

No one has a clue
But the rest of the girls
Pretending to be okay
Full of hate

Mostly for themselves
Not knowing how
To escape the crazy eights

Around the loops
Of hope and loss
The cost we pay is so high

Losing ourselves
Because no one taught us how not to

The Aftermath

55

-remember who you are-

Lesley Gorrell

Confused

I can't even understand
A world where this can be ignored

And Earth will keep spinning
As if we never felt it stop

Self-Loathing

How much can I hate myself?

So ugly
Imperfect
Impossible

Lesley Gorrell

Whispers

The waves of your words don't reach my ears
But I know you whisper them about me

My heart feels them
And your glances give you away

All I can do is hang my head in shame
Making myself invisible
When no one does it for me

Judged

You know who you are

Even if you feel lost
You know you're not everything they say

Lesley Gorrell

Suppressed

I don't think that really happened
Maybe I'm just imagining
My mind playing tricks on me

Or . . .
Maybe not
I feel it in my body
A memory

I never understood
How someone could say
They packed it all away
With no recollection

Except maybe the knowing
That something was wrong

But we store it somewhere
To make it through
Until it comes peering over the horizon

Little nudges
Knocking on our doors

Knock, knock, knock
It's time to come out
But not to play

It's time
To face what's emerging

Lesley Gorrell

Flashback

I like floating
I like flying
Outer space
No more crying

Peaceful now
All is done
Someday I'm going to be the one

Who gets to say I'm better than this
Who gets to feel eternal bliss
When I learn how to let this go
Once and for all

I can't wait for it to be over
No more looking over my shoulder
Under a rock or deep inside
Wherever it may be hiding

Just when I think there is no more
Here we go again
A new face, a new place
Reliving it

It's happening now
Right here in our bed
The aftermath of sex
Never would have expected you'd get to see it

Something like this
Firsthand
And yet you seem to understand

Watching me talking to someone else
Crying and writhing
Slowly subsiding

Until I fall to restless sleep
Still hanging on through the morning

That one was tough
A little rougher than the others I'd say
When will they go away?
Is this even mine to feel?

I don't know where he came from
I saw that place in a movie once
Does my mind just make them up?

I see them from every time
And every land
Speaking languages I don't understand
I'm always invisible
That I know for sure

Sometimes telling them no
Sometimes just going with the flow
Sometimes welcoming the burn

This . . . in my body
This is what I know
I feel the stories we carry
I guess I'm the one you can trust
To tell the world how they made us feel

Remnants

My arms
Up and over
Around my head
Ripping my shoulders

I wake up in the middle of the night that way

I hadn't really remembered that part
Funny how things get stuck

My neck
Holding the pain
Of the trauma I guess
It won't let me rest some days

Triggers
Taking me away
To far-off places

Different scenes
Of people on top of me
Draining my life with a blade
The victim of a man doing his deeds

Lesley Gorrell

It's always this way
Well, so far, that is
I wonder if I'll see something new soon

I'm kind of sad
But kind of not
Trying to figure all this out

It's a curious way to feel
Considering the memories

Of realms I've traveled
In this life or past
All stacked up

Same theme
And no reason
For any of it

Dissociating

It's not that bad
Dying here by your hand

My back against the table
Watching your knife
Pushing into my chest

Through the center
Perfect aim

I see the blood
Starting to run
Slow and warm

The scene is quiet
Full of Vikings

Old stone and wood
Damp and musty
No trust amongst the men
Just the bond of destruction

Silent tears
No fear
My heart aching for you

Lesley Gorrell

Why?
Why do you have to?
You don't even know
It is just the way

Sad
That I have to die here like this
But it's really not that bad

Your gleaming blade
The edges—softly rolling waves
The pattern perfectly etched
A beautiful relic

I can see your eyes shining
I can honor that you earned it
Feeling admired, respected

Puncturing through skin and bone
A satisfying task
Filling your empty spaces for now

I am beautiful
I am allowing

I am still
I am watching
I am loving you anyway

And I forgive you
I am not afraid
I am not lonely
I am not regretting
I am not resisting

It's just really not that bad

Tracers

Dissociation
When the light cascades
After the moving shapes

Do you know how much I can take
With all you put into me?
I can endure anything!

Parts of us
All over each other
My eyes as dizzy as my mind

But one more time
We'll go again
Do you know what it takes
To take you?

Splitting away
To the depths of my mind that scare me
Transported to a different world
Fast-forwarding through the maze
Where my thoughts are crazy

Let's turn this into a game

Go ahead, give me more
I know I can take it

All the power within me
I am the ultimate strength
Oh, how I hate you

Silent rage
Under this daze
I will break your fucking face one day

Feeling sideways
Twisted
Reality shifted

Knowing I'll be back someday
When this feeling passes

Lesley Gorrell

Surrender

I think I'll just cut it all away
I think I will just . . .
Surrender

I think I'll just lie down and go to sleep
Too tired to wave the flag
White, worn, sad

I think it's time to go home
Where I don't have to fight so hard
Waiting again for tomorrow

I think I just don't care anymore
I'm so weary

I think my heart no longer wants to beat
Always pounding through my chest
It needs a rest

I think my nerves will love the calm
They won't have to work so hard
To keep me hanging on

I think I want to watch the blood run
All over my face

And down my arms
And through my hair
And stand in it until the end

Relief is coming
My eyes are closed
The wet of it on my hands

I hate this part . . .
The smell of it!
I'm jolted back
My stomach turning

What have I done?
My heart still pounding
The anticipation becoming panic

Now I have to come back
And face the music

I just wanted to go away
From the pain
Just for a while

Lesley Gorrell

I just wanted to breathe
So softly
Escaping to a quiet place

I just want to know
I will not have to endure
Another lifetime of suffering

Surrender
Surrender
Time to go home

Cutting

It's not a game
Or attention-seeking
Just a little relief
No other reason

A release
So I can breathe
So I don't die all the way

One little breath
To keep me going
For just a little longer

Haven't you ever wondered why someone would do this?

It's kind of like everyone else
Looking for a way
To numb the pain

Or punish themselves
For not being any better

Lesley Gorrell

Self-Harm

I'm allowed to be this way
If it gets me through
One more day
Or years at a time

It isn't a crime, you know?
To want to feel better

Scarlet letters on my skin
Enticing you to mock me
Not really letters—
Just some lines from the blade

And those other times I burned instead
Cherry of my cigarette
Leaving circles
Dot to dot

What a plot this is turning out to be
It started when I was fourteen
Who knew it would follow me this long?

It's not a sin
To want to get through
Coping with abuse

It only hurts me, not you
So watch what comes flying out of your mouth
It might come back around

One day it could be your daughter
Or son or father
Who just doesn't know what else to do

Be glad it's not you

Lesley Gorrell

Tested

I like the pain
I deserve the blame

Punishment through this razor blade

I knew I was bad
I heard all along
This is all just a test I'm failing

The Artist

One, two, three
From the eye through the cheek
The blade drawn down both sides so they're equal

Looks like I was crying blood
Drug through the mud

It makes me sick being this way
Thin lines down my face
Six in place
I love how it looks in this moment

Proof that I'm bad
And the laughingstock that I am

Admiring my work
I can't believe the hurt that led me here

Maybe it's not so awful
I'm still here after all

Better than some
Who couldn't outrun the call
Back home to safety

Lesley Gorrell

Fighting is hard
The longest yard
And sometimes I just need a break
A sweet escape through this razor blade

My most trusted friend
It doesn't judge me in the end
Silently catching red tears from my chin
Wishing for me to be okay

Sorry for the moment I couldn't resist
Feels like bliss for just long enough
To get me through

Times are changing, I always say
I'm putting my collection away
Never going to reach for them again

Then the temptation comes
I like choosing which one
Can't let doubt set in
It ruins the fun

My wounds
A work of art
For the dearly departed
Why don't you have answers for me
When I'm pleading?

I need the truth
That always eludes me when I'm here

This place
In this bed
Carving scars into my face

Can't wait to hear the reviews
If anyone has a clue what I'm saying

The Reconciling

~remember who you are~

Lesley Gorrell

Ghosts

This is it
It has to be!
I want to be free from you!

Refusing Silence

No one wants to hear me
So I'll tell it to the world

Lesley Gorrell

Seeking

Once there was a girl
From a faraway land
Standing in front of me
In the mirror

Trying to say
It will all be okay
In the end

Not really an ending
Actually the beginning
Of whatever is coming
After this short appearance

Once I was a girl
Who wasn't so sad
And pissed at the whole fucking world
It wasn't so bad for a while

Not that I was ever happy
Always felt a little alone
Surrounded but on my own
In my head
Trying to sort out the order of things

Never prayed for wings to fly
Out of any place
Just sank down deep
Inside myself
Beginning the wait
Of whatever would be

I'm good at hanging on
Cemented in the suffering
Not moving a single muscle
But to clutch and hold my breath

Frozen in time
Frozen in my mind
Just waiting for what's next

Vexed
Cursed with not knowing
How to be any different

Obedient
Following instructions
Unable to think for myself

I'm finding out now
Seeking the answers
Gaining some clarity
Don't we all need it?

I do
For the stranger of a girl
I always wanted to be

The girl
Who really is just . . .
Me

Labeled

Beautiful, ugly girl
Trying to be more than who she is
Wishing she was different
Longing to be . . . beautiful
Oh, the things we try to hide from ourselves

What are you running from, dear?

Well, the fear . . .
Of not being good enough
For God knows who

Fear of anyone seeing the truth
Of what an ugly girl I am
I'll do anything to keep them from saying it

"Ugly"
Because I know it's true
Because I feel it through and through
Because people told me so
When I was still growing

Cutting to the core
Hot sword through my belly
Making me feel
Like a stain on this place
Not worthy of taking up space

"Beautiful"
"Ugly"
"Girl"
Does it matter?

The stickiness these labels put on me
Disguising the magnificent gifts within
Why do I listen?

Words that slice
How do we learn to deflect them?

All the wonder that unravels
The loud pound of the gavel
When they enter our ear

What our minds perceive
And the truth of us that lies beneath
I guess we need to experience both
Personal growth

How will we learn to hear ourselves
Over and above everyone else?

The journey to who we really are
No matter the appearance

Lesley Gorrell

Reflection

Ha, ha, ha!
In your face!
Fucking disgraced, looking at you

I hate this mirror
Reflecting what I feel
Ugly, unworthy
Tired of the journey

I think I'm going to be sick
I think I better run quick!
Far, far away from here

Hurry
Find something else to do
To distract yourself from the truth

You're not happy
With the way things are
You're going to be covered in more scars
If you don't get ahold of yourself

Maybe I'll write a book
Do a puzzle, learn to juggle
I don't fucking know

Can't let my head go
To the darkest places
It doesn't want to be

There's so much more here
For you to see

I just want to feel better
Maybe I'll write a letter
To anyone who would give a fuck
About how I feel

Hmm
Can't think of anyone
Who would want to hear any of this
Too much bullshit

Even I'm exhausted
Listening to myself
There's nothing new to tell

I guess that's why I'm always writing
The keyboard doesn't mind my typing

Lesley Gorrell

It's my forever friend
And sometimes the pen
When I want to feel the paper

A better friend than razor blades
Back in the good ol' days
When it felt so deviant to have them

My secret
My way to release
No one would get to know

Except when it's written all over me
For the whole world to see
And wonder who this crazy girl is

Ahhh, "crazy"
Disguising the pain
We are all in it
Our own way

The Cost

Fight, flight, freeze, fawn
My nervous system has won
Something's wrong with this moment

My body demands the reaction
No choice in my mode of survival

No opinion
No decision
Just happens
Automatically

Survival
Mine . . . not so fit
As messy as it gets
Because I keep choosing this

Somehow, I keep landing here
Scenarios of predator and prey

One day I'll learn
The part I play
Maybe get out of my own way

When I come to know
I run the show
Responsible for my experiences

Takes a long time to view things this way
With this interesting lens of understanding

It wasn't my fault
I didn't know better
Until I learned I can choose more for myself
It doesn't have to stay this way

And slowly I begin to build my strength
Courage and fury
To no longer worry what others think or need

Sacrificing myself to fill up the rest of humanity
How dare I say no to any request

No matter how great
No matter how small
I yield when they call

It's not an option to hurt someone's feelings
A thought I cannot bear
A consequence I shall not pay

Oh, but the price is so great in the end

Lesley Gorrell

Endings

To what end
Do I cry these tears?

All the years of suffering
Etching wounds into my skin
Trying to start over

To what end
Do I look ahead?

Desperately longing to escape the madness
And crushing pressure in my chest
Reaching for the rest of what life should really be

Not in this place
Not in this space

To what end
Do I allow my mind to consume my time upon the earth?

What is it worth?
The pain, the fear, the worry
Throwing away so many todays
Remembering how things used to be

Or imagining the future
What's the use?
It will never turn out that way

To what end
Am I always trying to wiggle my way out of the now?

I love when my head is in the clouds
But when I'm there the moments are fleeting

When will I learn to plant my feet hard onto the ground
Feeling joy in whatever can be found?

Only in the present
I get it
It's a long road to learn our lessons
And takes a lifetime to gain the awareness

Our essence
Used to scare us when we didn't really know

Then we come to be one with what is
We can feel eternal bliss
Even while still in our bodies
If we move the power away from our thoughts

Our brains working for survival
While our hearts are dying
The soul only begins thriving
When we loosen our grip

The river of life
Always flowing

Raging
Or slowing
Or seemingly still
Give up the will to control it

We can only watch or wade or swim
Navigating along the way
But all winding up in the same place
Getting to the end

Prompted

The suck
Embrace it
Get used to tasting it

> Get comfortable now
> With being uncomfortable
> You're gonna have to learn to live in it
> No gains will come if you keep running

What should I do now?

> Think about them saying "wow"
> You should have followed your dream
>
> Oh, what you could have been
> Oh, what you could have given
> With everything you've learned
>
> What a clever girl you are
> If only you had believed in yourself
> And what you have to offer the world
>
> You're going to have to stop hiding
> You're going to have to share your writing

Telling the stories
Of all of you
To everyone who will listen

Just begin
The rest will follow
You won't have to do it alone

The others will arrive
Standing by your side
And you won't be afraid anymore

Release it
And they will come
In love

Calling

Here you are
Just like I planned

Reading the words
You couldn't comprehend
When I spoke them

A force from inside
Pushed me
To write it all out

Here you are
Jaw on the floor
More than you can handle
The truth

The axe has fallen
Here is my calling
Spilling all my guts to the world

Hard to hear?
Nowhere near the nice girl you all know

Lesley Gorrell

Offering

Here is my darkness
So you can find your own
Shadows
Waiting to be discovered

And pulled up and out
For full release
So you can be free from yourself
And whatever else

Here is my pain
So you can gain understanding
Of everything inside you
Screaming for help and healing

Here are the lies
I once believed were true
So you can maneuver
In a different way too

Through the rest of your life
So it's not a total waste of time

It feels like it's always running out
Trying to decide what it's all about

The Thread

It's putting it out there
For others to hear
Connecting the dots
Of what we feel

I'm so tired right now
Typing these letters
Pulled out of bed
Putting it all together

To make some kind of sense
For when you read it
I know how much you need it

I did too
And waited so long
For it to come around
Needing more of
What I never found

Someone else to hear me say
I wasn't okay
Because neither were they

Every time I step away
I'm pulled back to this expression
To let you know
Words can be more than weapons

My eyes are heavy
But not my chest
I just want to rest

Not because I'm weary this time
Because I continue to write and cry
Releasing the words as they push out

Going back to read the lines
Going back in time
Or somewhere else
Or looking forward
I just can't ignore what comes
Into my mind
In an instant
Have to be ready to catch it

It's for me
It's for you
It's for anyone who needs the truth

Discovery

Everything they said was true
What my body already knew

That evil men would come for me
To punish me with their pain

I thought the messaging was to blame
Programmed to attract
All the bad things that happened

The grown-ups hoped to keep me safe
Maybe I could escape the doom
If the warnings took hold

Now I know my trajectory was set
At only five years old
When three angels came to comfort me
The terror too much to fathom

I can't believe I lived through it
I can't believe someone could do it
But now I see the truth

Lesley Gorrell

And new healing can begin
From the deepest parts within
That just weren't ready before

A feeling I couldn't ignore
Now that uncovered
So much can be explained

Trajectory

Did they even know
My mind was shouting no?
I wasn't prepared

Couldn't they see the look on my face
Desperate to be anywhere but here?

Weren't they aware of
What my stillness meant?
The silence screaming
"I don't want this!"

I wish I would have had a voice
I wish I knew I had a choice
Than to let these awful things happen
I just couldn't grasp it

Not knowing who I am
Or that I can make my own plan
For what I want
And how to feel
I don't have to surrender to everyone else

Lesley Gorrell

The weight
Of holding my breath
Waiting for what's next

Why did no one tell me
I can change my trajectory?

I didn't know I was worth anything more
Than doing what I'm told

I wish they'd raised me to be bold
It would be better than this old story

Of how people took things from me
That should only be shared in the safest places
Sacred spaces

What could I have been?
Something so different
Than a place for men to go
Because I let them

Forward

The line is drawn
In the sand
I can't go back again

Why do I keep punishing myself?
Hiding
Keeping my light from shining

Why do I hate this misery
But love its company?

Gravity
Not the only weight holding me down
I'm stuck in one place
Taking up space

Wishing to be useful
Wishing I could change the world
Still needing to change myself first

I can't go back
Don't you know
That I want to go everywhere with you
And hold you in my heart
And watch you start to light your own way?

The journey continues
I thought I was healed
Addicted to food now
Instead of the cutting that used to numb me

Deeper still
There is more to do
We're never done learning and growing
Finding the "knowing"

Tiny seeds
A few at a time
Opening my mind once again

There is no limit to our expanse
No matter how advanced we believe ourselves to be

Seek and ye shall find
As much as we can
Before our time here ends
Even make some new friends on our way

Today, the line is in the sand
I can't go back—understand?

I can't help you
Until I help myself
Not by punishing
But by loving

I've loved you
I love you still
We are parts of each other

Time to love me
The way I love you

Lesley Gorrell

Note to Self

I can love you better than this

I can take greater care
Than hating
And punishing
And never believing you're enough

Every time you needed me
I just agreed you were lost
And broken
And weak
And awful

And fat
And ugly
And stupid

Disgusting
You never should have trusted me

Acceptance

All marked up from your self-mutilation

It can't be erased
I will have to take you as you are

Lesley Gorrell

Growth

More than my pain
More than the game
Of pretending I'm not worthy

To speak my name
To stand in my strength
And say what I have to say
To the world

A girl
Finding her way
To a woman unfolding

Gift

I hate my voice
Reading aloud
The way it sounds

And the way it feels
Pushing up and out
Maneuvering through my mouth

Uncomfortable
Quivering inside
I'm used to hiding
I understand why

Not even I want to listen
These words
Better left written

My silent gift
To the world

Lesley Gorrell

Prophetic

We don't have to treat each other
This way anymore

This is the beginning
For all to win
When we learn a new way

Healing ourselves
Invites the others
To open their ears
And their eyes
And their hearts
To see us all as equal

I don't know how it's going to look
But I'm going to write the book
For all of us

The Awakening

~remember who you are~

Lesley Gorrell

Melody

My heart song
No notes to play along
Just the words
As they come calling

I have so much to say
For you and for me—
Our feelings of longing
For freedom

No obligation to fake it
No reason to make believe you're okay
I'll hold the space

A few safe moments
For you
To dwell . . .
On what runs deep
And through and underneath
The things we hide behind

I'm lending you my voice
To help you move along

A path to finding and feeling
Your wholeness
When no one else is watching

I've got you now
Are you ready to begin?

Listen now
For the song of your soul
However it may come

You're the only one who can hear
What's for you

Who cares if they don't understand
We all have our own plan
We made it before we came
To pave our way

You already have permission
To embrace your authenticity
And unearth all the gifts within

Lesley Gorrell

I know it seems hard
I know you're guarded
I know you've started so many times
To try to feel better

Let's go together
I'll hold your hand
I'll never let you stand alone

Or lie to yourself
Or believe
That there will never be more

I hear a melody
Leading me by the heart
I don't know where
But it's a start

Trusting it will take me
To places I'm supposed to be
For whatever reason

I'm writing the words
That will give me the voice
That's been buried

My words
My choice to share
So we can be together
Finding our way
Through the darkness

Lesley Gorrell

By Your Side

I'm by your side
As darkness falls
When all is lost

Sitting with you
Your weakest hour
Lending you my power

Last shred of strength
To hold on one more day
Hold, hold, hold
Until the light peers through again

It's okay if you're needing
To feel the pain
When you can't move or speak or breathe

Or see any way
Beyond this moment
But hold, hold, hold

I'm by your side
When you're on the floor
Broken, grasping
For any fucking relief

I can't believe the places we go
To escape

You will not hear my voice
You will not feel my touch
It's just too much

When you can't even think of healing
When you can't fathom your own feelings

I will not push
I will not prompt
I will not ask or try to explain

I will not tell you it will be okay
That's for another day
Just hold, hold, hold

I'm here
By your side
So you'll hang on
Long enough for things to change
New breeze blowing your way

Sun on your face
Hope in your heart
Maybe a new start

And the walls will thin
And the shield will heavy
Maybe ready to lay it down

Tired from carrying
The greatest weight
Wanting to be free

I'm here
With you in this moment
Holding, holding, holding
This sacred space

Here with you
I won't leave your side
Hold, hold, hold
Just one more day

Enough

I'm enough
Exactly this way
Understand what I'm saying?

Yeah, you
Little girl in my mirror

I wish I could recognize
Or believe in her

Who do you think you are?

I guess . . .
I just want to be loved

By who more than anyone else?

Myself I would say
Don't we all feel that way?

Why do you think it's so hard?

Because I'm scarred
All over my heart
All over my body

Because I had to take the pain
Out on myself
I never wanted to hurt anyone else
And it was too much to hold

The weight that we carry
Needs to be released
We all find outlets
Mostly reckless

Mirror, mirror
Facing myself
The ultimate exposure
Vulnerable

Oh, yes
We must see
All the ugly parts
And learn to love and honor
The whole person

That includes
The whole fucking mess
We are desperate to hide

Why do we need to be seen a certain way?
Like we have it all together
Like we do it better
Than everyone else

But longing to connect
Could we ever let down our guard

I want to know you
I want to nurture your struggles
And honor mine

I want to sit
In a sacred circle
Where heart songs are shared
And we declare our bold visions have reason

And that we are enough
For ourselves and each other—
Just the way we are

Lesley Gorrell

Unapologetic

Who do I want to be?
Who do *I* want to be?

Unapologetically me
But
Mostly concealing my truth

Deep ugliness keeps me hiding
From myself and everyone else

Striving for freedom
My word
Year after year
I don't need the bracelet to remind me

It's seared in my brain
Maybe someday
I'll get there

What exactly am I waiting for?
I'm the only one
Holding me back
Afraid to step out
Where someone will see me

No one wants to be judged
Especially an ugly girl
Who wants to feel pretty

And vibrant and strong
And on top of the world
The full energy of life
And all that it offers

No one wants to hear you
Sit down, silly girl
Who are you for the light to shine on?

That's not nice!
No one wants to be reminded
They should stay in the dark

Who do I want to be?
Who do *I* want to be?
Just me!

Me
Without being sorry for it
I just don't want to hold myself back anymore
I want to embrace all that's in store for me

I'm never going to live
If I keep myself quiet
I'm never going to reach the sun
That I long to feel warming my face
When I'm not afraid to take up space

Who do you want to be, little girl?

I want to be the woman I've become
To move through space
With a smile on my face

Smiling for myself
A real smile from within
Not the socially acceptable grin
That's been plastered on my face
Every day
So the rest of the world will think I'm okay

Why do I have to be okay for *them*?
Why do we all have to look like we're winning?
Why is it not okay to say it
When we're not?

I'm going to say it
I'm going to say it for all of us
It's okay to not be okay every goddamned day

It's okay that I feel this way
I shouldn't have to be afraid
For my secrets
To be discovered

I want to feel beautiful and alive
And to be my best
Not suffering this emotional death

Secrets
Secrets
Why do we keep them?
They separate us, you know?

When all we want is to be together
We all want to feel like part of the whole
We all want to let go
Of our shame

Aren't we the same?
I think most of us are
Wanting to be loved
Wanting to be heard—
Permission to share our gifts with the world

To feel whole and worthy
And honor our journeys
Out in the open
With the wind in our hair
It's exhilarating when we let ourselves fly

Alive . . .
Alive!!!
Sun on my skin
Breath in my lungs
Comfort in the space my body holds
I can love myself
I can love myself fully

Okay, I've decided
I'm going to be who I came here to be
Unapologetically me
I don't need permission
From anyone on this earth

I already have it
The light of the universe is in me
And all the rest

The Source of our existence
The human experience
The Thread—
Connecting us all

Lesley Gorrell

Familiar

I know you
I see you moving through

One voice
One breath
One step

One reason
It's you

Keep believing
It's coming soon

Hard to Hear

The hardest things—
No one wants to hear them

The hardest truths
Need to be spoken
So they lose their hold

I know it's uncomfortable
But, here we are
Sisters, daughters, mothers
Here to declare
We have found each other

Joining together to stand and say
"No more of this, there's a better way"

We are going to be the teachers
We are going to make them believers

We will no longer have to hide our pain
We will no longer live in shame
They will stop demanding
That we are to blame

They will start to understand
That we were *not* wrong and it's *not* our fault
That we did *not* ask for what we got

Exactly what was coming to us
For not doing whatever it was
That would have stopped it

"No more, no more of this!"
We're going to get this fixed
We're tired of the societal bullshit
That keeps us hating ourselves

It's going to be our turn soon
We are coming for you

All the way
Loud and clear
You won't have a choice but to hear
The hardest things

Anthem

Everything we feel
If only it weren't real
For so many of us

Everything we say
That puts us in the way
Of ourselves

Everything we lost
Whatever the price
We paid it

Everything we gained
By staying one more day
When we could have gone

All that has been endured
Every cut from every word
We are now healing

All the emptiness in our eyes
All the burning we feel inside
All the rage kept alive
By reliving it

Lesley Gorrell

Cursing the way
We let ourselves
Continue to play the game

Unable to move
Wanting so badly
To escape

We only could in our minds
How powerful a thing . . .

We are going to believe a different way
Moving through the rest of our days
Free

Free!
From everything we can possibly blame
From suffering, despair
And blissful dreams of the end

Free from wanting to just be done
Free from thinking they were the ones
When it was us

Everything we feel
Is going to be better
Than we ever imagined it could be

Everything we will meet
Without the defeat we once felt

Our arms and hearts so wide open
Embracing the world
Sharing what we now know

Love and comfort
Forgiving and trusting
The way we were going was meant to be
To find each other now
And teach the rest

Transforming ourselves and the world
To make this a better place
For all

We just didn't understand
We are here
To teach each other

All here now
A collective voice
For hope and change
No longer a slave to old ways

Now our job to light the way
Elevation to a higher plane
I can't wait for us all to feel it

Destination

Are all these wounds
Really the gift
That will bring us closer?

A reason to connect
And share
And move through

Walking onward
Hands and arms
Locked together
Finding the best parts of ourselves
In each other

To shine our light
For the world
So the others can see
And come too?

Let's go
Let's go to the place
That is open
To freedom and loving
And carving the path

Lesley Gorrell

Come with us
So you can see
The choice

Finding your way again
All is not lost

It's the beginning
Of finding the strength
That will get you through
The rest of it

Summit

I'm talking to you
The girl who's crawling inside herself
Trying to be invisible
And silent
The violence has paralyzed you

For what it's worth
I've walked in your shoes
I know what you've been through
It's why I'm here
To sing to you
The songs of my soul

I'm talking to you
The part that longs to be free
I'm talking to who
You think you are now
Lost but finding your way

You won't feel it
In this moment
But we will meet at the summit one day
After we have climbed our climbs
Transcended

Lesley Gorrell

I can't wait to hold your hands
And you'll know someone understands

Yeah, I'm talking to you
I'll see you soon

Glimpse

You're going to light the way
To better days
For so many

You're going to write the book
That gives the words
To those who can't yet speak

You're going to love them so much
They come to say
They love you too

And healing will begin
And the day will be won

Teaching the masses
How it could be
To set themselves free

Lesley Gorrell

Invitation

Standing
In my truth
How about you?

Would you like to come along?
Our heart songs colliding
A choir for the masses?

No free passes
We all must face the music

If you're ready
Come with me
It's going to be amazing

Together

Journey

Worthy

Us

Lesley Gorrell

Rhetoric

What can I say?
Time gone by

Dreams, lost by not acting
On what I know
To be my truth

I do solemnly swear
To find her again
The warrior princess within me

My strength, my vision, my love
I'm driven to share with the world
Messages in my soul

I hereby declare
I will do what it takes
To teach the lessons of my heart
To anyone willing to listen

Who can I tell?

Everyone
Some will receive and some will not
Don't get distraught by the naysayers

Hold the line
It will come in time
What you wish for

How do I say it?

With your whole heart
And loving and guiding
And sharing what you have learned

Generosity, passion, authority
Over what is yours
No one can take it away

How will I know?

Listen within
Then begin

I don't know what direction!

Start with reflection
Deep in you are the answers

Lesley Gorrell

Find the quiet place
And be open to what comes
You are the one meant to hear
What is for you

Yours
Yours alone
As much as you will allow
To come through
When you clear the space

What can we do?
Each of us
Listen for the beat of our drum
Follow it down the path it is leading
So we know what to say

Takeoff

Pieces of me
All over the place
God's looking at the mess

Get up, little girl
Stop thinking you're a waste of space
You're going to have to decide
Where to go from here

What happens now?
Which way will you go?

On forever
Wondering what I could have been
Wanting to win it all

Take the leap
He told you so
You heard it from your heart

Be free
Heal
Move
Breathe
Grow

Lesley Gorrell

Find the path
No one can carry your torch
Step forward and light your own way

You are not stuck
You must choose to move ahead
Only then will you see

You must keep moving
The only way to save yourself
And share with them

> Keep going now
> Step out and I will show you
>
> Do you trust me?
> Listen closely
>
> I'm ready
> To watch you fly

~remember who we are~

GRATITUDE

Thank you for sharing this space with me. Thank you for being open to all that is possible when we begin healing.

Thank you to those who came before us to pave the way—so that we may stand unapologetically in our truths.

Thank you for choosing understanding and grace. Thank you for remembering that we are individual, yet we are one.

I'm grateful for our shared humanity—the thread that connects us all.

About the Author

For years, LESLEY GORRELL lived in silence. She felt invisible, disconnected, and consumed by suffering. When healing became the only way forward, she began writing as a lifeline—documenting her thoughts, tracing her pain, and slowly reclaiming her voice. That voice is now a force for others. As a writer, author, and advocate, Lesley creates spaces of truth, courage, and emotional restoration. *The Thread* is a testament to survival and a call to those who long to feel less alone.

Her lived experience with abuse, self-harm, and identity loss informs every word she writes, honoring the wound and moving toward wholeness.

Poems by Title

www.ingramcontent.com/pod-product-compliance
Lightning Source LLC
Chambersburg PA
CBHW031130130726
47988CB00006B/2310